Quilts for Beginners 1
Make Your First Quilts

By Felicity Walker

Get Felicity's free newsletter at
QuiltersDiary.com

ISBN: 1494764768
ISBN-13: 978-1494764760

Contents

1/ Make Your First Quilt Today!

THIS BOOK IS for anyone who would like to learn more about quilting and how to make that first quilt.

Have you ever feasted your eyes on the beautiful fabric at your local crafts store and wished you knew how to make something with all those glorious colors and prints? Have you ever thought a quilt would be the perfect present for someone you care about, if you only knew how to make one? Does quilting seem like it might be fun, but you're not sure how to get started?

I was in your shoes once. I remember how intimidated I felt by all the mysterious tools and techniques quilters seemed to need. I felt uncomfortable visiting my local quilt shop because I thought everyone there knew all about quilting, while I didn't know anything. I was afraid to ask stupid questions.

But I really loved fabric, and I liked making things with my hands, so I plunged in and made my first quilt without any help at all. It was a twin-size bed quilt. I bought hundreds of purple fabric squares on eBay and laboriously sewed them together, one by one. In spite of my ignorance, the quilt ended up looking good! We still use it at our house. But because I started quilting all on my own, I did a lot of things the hard way.

I have learned a lot more about quilting since then. In more than fifteen years at the sewing machine and ten years of writing about quilting for a major crafts publisher, I've discovered all kinds of shortcuts and simple techniques that make quilting faster, easier and more fun. The purpose of this book is to pass on what I've learned to you, so you don't have to learn quilting the hard way. You will start out knowing all the quilting secrets it took me years to discover.

All you need to make your first quilt is this guide, some fabric, and a few basic tools and supplies. You can actually make a whole

©2015 QuiltersDiary.com

quilt—a beautiful quilt you can be proud of—in just a day or two. Everything you need to know is right here. I predict that you will be amazed by how easy quilting is. You may be even more amazed by how good your first quilt looks. Most of all, you'll love how much fun it is to make something useful and beautiful using your own hands and your own creative instincts.

Once you find out how easy quilting is, and how much everyone enjoys snuggling up in your first creation, you'll want to make another quilt, and then probably a few more!

Quilts make wonderful special-occasion gifts. (Nothing says "love" quite like a soft, warm, cuddly homemade quilt.) I've given quilts to new babies, to high school and college graduates, to newlyweds, and even to friends who were going through a hard time. All were deeply appreciated. Seeing the delight on the face of the lucky recipient when you give a quilt is a wonderful reward for your time and effort.

Many quilters also donate their creations to charity. Some quilters even make money selling their quilts or finishing quilts for other people. Quilting really can be a lifelong creative journey.

It's a great privilege for me to help you get started.

I'd like to invite you to join my mailing list at QuiltersDiary.com. I will send you a handy free guide to standard quilt and mattress sizes, just for signing up. You will also receive my free newsletter with tips on quilting techniques, tutorials on how to make favorite quilt blocks, quilted holiday projects, and much more. I'm also available to answer quilting questions.

What's Inside this Book?

Everything you need to know to make your first quilt is here:

❖ A brief history of quilts and overview of the most popular types of quilting.

❖ Overview of quilt fabric, batting, threads, and the essential quilting tools and supplies you will need to get started. (Don't worry – you don't need to spend a fortune.)

❖ Step-by-step guide to the basics of cutting, sewing, quilting, and finishing your quilt, with lots of photos to show you exactly what to do.

❖ Complete quilt patterns and step-by-step photo instructions for making the three quick and easy quilts shown below:

Project #1: Quilt-as-you-go Table Runner

Quilt-as-you-go is one of the very easiest and fastest ways to make a quilt. Once you make this quick table runner, you will be able to apply the quilt-as-you-go technique to quilts of any size.

Project #2: Easy Rail Fence Quilt

Rail Fence is a classic quilt that helps you learn about selecting fabrics that work well together, cutting them, and sewing quilt blocks together. You can give this quilt a lot of different looks by simply choosing different fabrics.

Project #3: Double-Four-Patch Baby Quilt

This quilt is based on the Four-Patch quilt block, a traditional favorite and one of the essential blocks any quilter should know. It may look a bit complicated, but it is actually a lot easier to make than it looks!

For each quilt, you will get the complete pattern, a list of how much fabric you need, and start-to-finish instructions for planning, cutting, sewing, and completing the quilt. I'll walk you step by step through the whole process, again with plenty of photos to show you just what to do.

Because you choose the fabrics, the quilts you will make from these patterns are unique. No one else's quilt will be quite like yours. The color and design of your quilt will have your own personal stamp. The fabrics you choose can be as bold and colorful, or as soft and serene as you want.

So let's get started!

What is a Quilt?

A quilt is two layers of fabric with an insulating layer of batting (also called wadding) in between.

Quilters call these three layers the "quilt sandwich." The top layer of the sandwich is the decorated part of the quilt, the part you ordinarily see. The middle layer is there mainly to provide warmth, but also to give depth to your stitching. The back layer of the sandwich protects the batting. All three layers are held together by stitching, which can be sewn either by hand or by machine. The act of sewing the layers together is called quilting.

Quilts come in all styles, from traditional patterns that wouldn't look out of place in George Washington's parlor, to abstract art quilts that hang in museums of modern art.

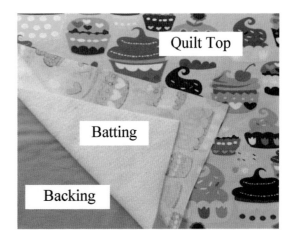

Quilt Top

Batting

Backing

The Different Types of Quilts

There are three basic kinds of quilts:

Pieced. A pieced quilt is assembled by sewing together cut pieces of fabric. This is called "piecing" in the quilting world. If you look closely at the photo below, you can see the lines between the different pieces that went into this Drunkard's Path quilt.

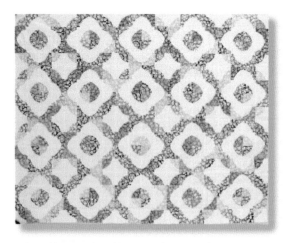

Appliqué. Appliqué is the art of sewing decorative elements onto the quilt top. Appliqué elements can be stitched onto the quilt by hand or with a sewing machine. The flowers and stems in this photo were appliquéd onto a white background fabric:

Whole cloth. A whole-cloth quilt is made from a large, plain piece of fabric. Traditionally, the only decoration on this kind of quilt is the fancy stitching that quilts the layers together. I don't recommend this style for beginners, although you can buy whole cloth quilt tops that are pre-printed with stitching patterns to show you exactly where to sew.

For most people, making a small pieced quilt is the easiest way to learn about quilting. That's why this book focuses on pieced quilts. Even if you decide to try another kind of quilting, the skills you learn making your first pieced quilt will still come in handy.

Whatever type of quilting you decide you want to try, you need to know some basic skills. You will also need a few essential tools to get started. Having the right tools and a bit of knowledge will help you enjoy quilting more and help you really understand how to make lovely quilts.

2/ A Brief History of Quilting

QUILTS ORIGINATED AS a way to keep warm in the cold, unheated bedrooms of the past.

Fabric was scarce and expensive in earlier centuries, so women saved scraps from worn clothing, sacks from animal feed, old blankets, and other fabrics. They sewed the scraps together until they were large enough to cover a bed. An insulating layer of wool made the quilt warmer. You might call quilting one of the original forms of recycling!

Quilting made its way to America and Australia with European immigrants. Fabric was even more scarce and expensive in pioneer lands than it had been in Europe, so women used quilting to turn their fabric scraps into clothing and bedding.

Even in those early days, women used quilts to show off their fine stitching. It took many hours of laborious hand work to create a quilt back then, and quilters took pride in making their work beautiful. Some of the quilts made to celebrate important life events such as births or marriages were masterworks of the stitcher's art, like the Baltimore Album quilt in the bottom left column of this page.

The development of machine looms at the end of the 18th century made cotton fabric less expensive and more available to quilters. During the 19th century, new dyeing methods made bright reds and other brilliant colors available for the first time. Quilters no longer had to make do with leftovers from the rag bin, although many quilts were still made from recycled fabrics.

At the same time that fabric became easier to find, society's growing wealth provided women with more free time. Quilting became a hobby for middle-class women. Patchwork quilts grew more elaborate. Quilters started making some quilts purely for display, not just to provide warmth. The first quilts made purely as art were the crazy quilts of the Victorian era, which used silks and velvets to show off the maker's fancy stitches.

Victorian homes were adorned with crazy quilt patchwork throws, cushions, and tea cozies. This quilt from 1885 is a good example of the crazy quilt style:

Quilting and other forms of hand work began to go out of fashion in the early twentieth century, as commercially manufactured quilts started to compete with home-made quilts. With more women joining the workplace, it was easier and felt more "modern" to buy a manufactured quilt rather than put in the many hours it took to make one at home. Like other traditional crafts, quilting began to seem outdated in a world of cars, radios, and industrialized design.

Around the time of the American Bicentennial in 1976, a new wave of interest in reconnecting with the past brought quilting and other hand crafts back to popularity. Quilting fever has been growing ever since.

Today's quilter has it much easier than her cousins of previous centuries. Cutting fabric with scissors was slow and difficult, but today's quilters have rotary cutters and even fabric cutting machines to make the job fast and easy. Stitching was once done entirely by hand. Today's computerized sewing machines make it easy to sew accurately and create beautiful quilting designs at the touch of a button.

Improved batting, new speed-piecing methods, even fabric that comes pre-cut into shapes that are ready to sew—all these innovations have made quilting easier and faster than ever before. Fabric designed and made especially for quilting is available in a rainbow of colors and prints. Helpful tutorials abound on You Tube. There has never been a better time to learn to quilt.

Quilters are still proud of their craft's original thrifty ethic. Many modern sewists still use scraps cut from old clothes they have gathered from thrift stores or saved from other quilt projects. The quilt below was made with scrap fabrics.

Today, quilting is a huge business around the world, worth an estimated $26 billion per year. Quilts come in all sizes, shapes, and styles. They are made by crafters in the United States, Europe, Australia, Japan, and many other countries.

You can make a quilted postcard to send through the mail, a small art quilt to hang on your wall, quilted purses and clothing, quilts to snuggle up in while you watch TV, and of course, bed quilts to keep you warm while you sleep. It's easy to find reproduction fabric in the styles that were popular during the Civil War, the 1930s Depression era, or the 1950s – or to design your own original fabric and print it out from your computer.

Once you learn the basic skills of quilting, you'll find you've opened a world of unlimited creativity.

3/ Fabric for Quilting

FEASTING YOUR EYES on the gorgeous fabrics available today, choosing your favorite colors and prints, and making your fabric into something beautiful is one of the great joys of being a quilter.

Most of the quilt fabric you will find at a fabric or quilting store is made from 100% cotton. Cotton is relatively inexpensive, easy to sew, durable, creases easily, and washes well, so that's where we will start.

Of course, cotton isn't the only fabric used for quilting: there are many quilters who sew with wool and silk. Eco-friendly bamboo fabric is rapidly becoming more popular. But wool and silk are expensive, and require special handling when washed. Bamboo fabric is still something of a specialty item. Cotton fabrics are available in an almost infinite variety of colors and prints. You can find them everywhere. Cotton is still king, as far as most quilters are concerned.

Many quilt stores also stock cotton/polyester blends. I've quilted with cotton blends that I got from the thrift store. Call me a snob, but I prefer the feeling and durability of high-quality, natural-fiber fabric to any synthetic I've come across.

Is Fabric Quality Important?

When you buy fabric, as with many things, you get what you pay for. Cheap quilting fabrics have thinner threads. They are less tightly woven than high-quality fabrics, and

have more weaving flaws. The dyes used to manufacture them are less colorfast, and may bleed when they get wet. Cheaper fabric doesn't last as long or wear as well as more expensive, higher-quality fabric.

All that being said, not every quilt needs to last a lifetime. It probably doesn't make sense to spend a fortune on fabric for a toddler's drag-around quilt, which is guaranteed to get stained and worn and will no doubt be washed often. But please don't skimp on the fabric for your granddaughter's wedding quilt. The time you devote to making a special quilt like that is priceless. Make your time count by using high-quality materials.

Where can you find good-quality fabric? Look no further than your local quilt store. Chain stores, which compete on price, tend to stock lower grade fabrics. In fact, many fabric manufacturers make two lines of the same fabric designs: a lower grade product that goes to chain stores, and a higher-grade version that goes to the quilt shops. The best fabric is often called "quilt shop quality." There are also online fabric retailers who stock quilt-shop grade fabrics.

Fabric Grain

Most quilt fabric has a right side and a wrong side. The pattern looks richer and more detailed on the right side, and paler and fuzzier on the wrong side. Most of the time you will want to use the right side of the fabric, but there are times when the "wrong" side has just the shade you want. Don't feel shy about using it if you want to.

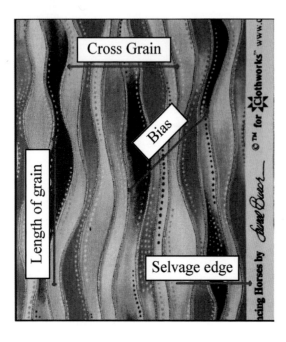

Fabric also has a grain. When the fabric is woven, the threads run in two directions — vertically and horizontally. The two sets of threads running at right angles to each other are called the straight of grain.

The threads that run parallel to the selvages are called the length of grain. Length of grain edges don't stretch much at all if you pull on them. The threads that run across the quilt are called the cross grain. Cross grain edges are a bit stretchier than the length of grain, but still not very stretchy.

The bias is an imaginary line that runs at a 45-degree angle across the fabric. Bias is important because when you cut angled shapes out of quilt fabric, you create a bias (45-degree) edge that is much stretchier than edges on the straight of grain. Bias edges must be treated with special care while you cut, sew, and press them, to avoid stretching your fabric out of shape. You don't have to worry about that with the quilts you will make from this book, though.

There is usually a woven white strip along each side of a length of quilt fabric. These edges are called the selvage. Most quilters trim off the selvages before working with the fabric. (Some quilters also collect the selvages and make scrap quilts out of them!)

Prewashing Quilt Fabric

Should you prewash new fabric before you quilt with it? Some quilters prewash every scrap of fabric. Others say it's a waste of time. Prewashing does add a couple of extra steps to the quilting process.

Here's my take on prewashing: if the quilt you are making will be washed in the future, then it's a smart idea to prewash your fabric before cutting and sewing it. Prewashing shrinks the fabric, so your quilt won't shrink and possibly get distorted after you finish making it.

Some art quilts and wall quilts will never be washed. Those quilts can safely be made with fabric that hasn't been prewashed.

Some fabrics, especially cotton flannels, shrink a LOT. Those fabrics should definitely be washed before you use them. I prewash flannels twice.

Certain fabrics tend to bleed dye, especially the darker, richer reds, browns, and blues. I've bought some fabric that bled so badly that I ended up throwing it away. Pre-testing the fabric alerts you to the danger that a particular fabric might stain others when you put it into a quilt.

Quilting teacher Laura Nownes tests suspicious fabrics by cutting a small square of the colored fabric and swirling it around in a glass of water with a square of white fabric. If either the water or the white fabric takes on a tinge of color from the colored fabric, you know the colored fabric is likely to bleed.

If you *really* love the bleeding fabric, you can treat it with a dye fixative called Retayne, which is designed to work on commercially printed fabric. In most cases, I would give the suspicious fabric a pass. It's a terrible feeling to see a stain on the new quilt you just spent many hours making.

How to Prewash Fabric

How should you prewash? Here's what I do.

1. Separate lights from darks.

2. Put like-colored fabrics together in the washing machine, on the shortest delicate cycle, using a very small amount of normal laundry detergent. (Some quilters prefer to use Woolite® or Orvus® soap, which is formulated especially for quilts. Some quilters don't use soap at all.)

3. After washing, check for colorfastness. If I see any color bleeding at this point, I rinse out the offending fabric with a little soap by itself. A fabric that bleeds the second time around is discarded—it will likely bleed on your quilt, and who wants that?

2. If the dyes seem stable, throw the fabrics in the dryer. Any shrinkage that will happen takes place in the dryer.

3. Fold each piece of fabric and put it away until you're ready to use it. When you're ready to quilt, press the fabric before you work with it to remove any wrinkles.

Fabrics for Quilt Backings

On most quilts, the top layer is the one that gets all the attention. The back side of the quilt is rarely seen, or never seen at all if the quilt hangs on a wall. Many quilters use fabric in a quilt backing that is plainer than the fabrics they use for the top. (This is starting to change – I see more and more quilters piecing the backs of their quilts with the same care as the tops.)

Quilting fabric tends to be about 42" wide, so if your quilt is wider than that, you will need a backing wider than one width of fabric.

One way to back a wide quilt is to buy special 108"-wide backing fabric. This used to be hard to find, but more and more quilt stores and online fabric retailers stock the extra-wide fabric now. I also see a proliferation of patterns and colors in extra-wide fabric.

A much cheaper approach is to use a bed sheet as backing fabric. This used to be frowned on because sheets are more densely woven than quilting fabric, and can be difficult to pierce with the needle if you hand quilt. But today's sewing machines are tough. I've quilted with sheets and been happy with the results. Buying a good sheet at a discount store is often less expensive than buying quilting fabric. It's even cheaper if you can find a good sheet at a thrift store.

If you want to make a wide backing from standard-width quilting fabric, you will need to piece the backing together. See Chapter 7 for detailed instructions on how to piece together a simple backing.

Working with Fabric Colors and Prints

One of the things that many new quilters struggle with is working out which colors and fabrics look good together. The use of colors in quilting is one of those subjects on which scholarly quilters have written many books. One of the best I know is *Color Play*, by Joen Wolfrom.

As you play with fabric, you will find that you have a natural affinity for certain colors and color combinations. You will also notice that you instinctively dislike other colors and combinations. The more you quilt, the more you will understand your own sense of color and know when to reach outside your color habits to try something new. The great thing is that there are no color police! You can try out any color combinations you want to.

For beginning quilters, I offer just a few color guidelines:

- **Use a variety of light, medium, and dark fabrics** in your quilts. Contrast between lights and darks makes a quilt interesting.

- **Use a mixture of small, medium, and large prints.** If you use all tiny prints, your quilt will look dull. If you use all large-scale prints, your quilt will look chaotic.

- **Try to match the scale of your prints to the size of the pieces you are sewing** in the quilt. Large-scale prints work well when cut into big pieces. But if you cut large prints into tiny pieces, they look completely different and the print may not make sense any more as a design. Conversely, tiny prints can look dull and washed out when cut into large pieces.

Compare the large-scale and small-scale prints on the right. They are both floral prints, but imagine how different a quilt would look made with the big William Morris flowers than it would if you used the tiny pastel roses. It's something to think about when you choose your fabrics.

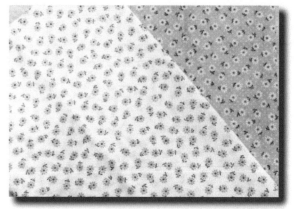

When you go fabric shopping, look for a mixture of colors and patterns that strikes a happy medium between light and dark, small and large. Your quilts will look better if you do.

One way to have some fun picking colors is to go to a paint store and pick up some of the color swatch cards that paint manufacturers provide, free of charge, for do-it-yourselfers who want to repaint their houses.

Look for the color cards that show combinations of several coordinating colors. While these cards are designed to help you pick out a color scheme for painting a room, they work just as well for quilts! When you go out fabric shopping, take your favorite color swatches with you and pick quilt fabrics that most closely match the ones you like from the swatch cards.

4/ Thread, Batting, and Tools

QUILTING THREAD, LIKE fabric, comes in different levels of quality. As with fabric, high-quality thread is more expensive than low-quality thread.

To my mind, better thread is always worth the extra investment. There are several major penalties for using poor-quality thread (and I suffered through them all before seeing the light):

- Your thread is more likely to break while you try to sew with it.

- Cheap thread throws off a lot of lint that gradually clogs up your sewing machine with dust.

- Cheap thread will not wear as well over the life of your quilt.

Thread comes in a variety of different types for different kinds of sewing.

Thread for machine piecing. For sewing fabric pieces together into a quilt top, I recommend a 40- or 50-weight cotton thread. I use Aurifil thread, but there are a number of other good brands. Ask your quilt store what they recommend. They will help you find the correct weight for what you want to sew.

For piecing, you don't usually want the thread to show through the fabric. A neutral color like off-white, beige or pale gray will blend in unobtrusively with just about every fabric color.

Thread for machine quilting. To sew the quilt layers together, a 40- or 50-weight cotton or polyester thread works well. I use YLI or Superior brand polyester quilting thread. Steer clear of rayon or metallic threads, which tend to break. We'll talk later about choosing the right color thread for quilting the layers.

Thread for hand quilting. If you want to piece or quilt by hand, look for thread labeled specifically for hand quilting. It is thicker than machine thread, and comes coated with a glaze or wax to make it slide easily through the fabric. Don't use hand quilting thread in your sewing machine.

If you have bought thread of unknown age at yard sales, or inherited thread from an older quilter, I'm sorry to say that you should not use that thread to make new quilts. Thread gets brittle as it ages. Invest in a new spool of thread for your next quilt.

Quilt Batting (Wadding)

Batting, called wadding in some parts of the world, is the insulating material that forms a quilt's middle layer. Depending on the batting you use, your quilt can be thin and cool, or thick and warm. The warmth of batting is determined by the type and thickness of the fiber in the batting.

Batting is manufactured in two basic ways: by needle punching, where thousands of needles pound through the fibers and lock them together into a sheet, or by covering the fibers with a thin layer of bonding agent called a scrim that keeps the fibers in place. Here are some of the most popular types of batting quilters use today:

- **Polyester.** Light and lofty, polyester batting makes a warm and snuggly quilt. Some quilters don't like working with polyester because it is a synthetic material. A thick polyester batting can have a tendency to billow up and fight you when you try to get it under the needle of your sewing machine. Thinner polyesters are easier to work with. Polyester washes and dries well.

- **Cotton.** Thin and relatively heavy, cotton shows off machine stitching well and washes well. Cotton batting isn't very warm.

- **Wool.** Warm and light but more temperamental to wash than cotton, wool batting is popular with show quilters because it shows off their fancy stitching so beautifully. There are new washable wool battings that make a wool quilt much easier to handle. Moths like to eat wool, so you need to be careful how you store it.

- **Bamboo.** A newcomer to the batting scene, bamboo is thin like cotton, but lighter than cotton and wonderfully soft. Many quilters like it because bamboo is grown without the use of pesticides, unlike cotton. Some quilters complain that bamboo tends to beard, or pull through the outer fabric when the quilting needle goes through it. I've machine quilted with bamboo and haven't had this problem.

- **Silk.** Silk is expensive and needs special washing, but quilters who make quilted clothing say there's nothing like silk for its beautiful, soft drape. Silk batting is thin, very light, and warm for its weight.

This list only scratches the surface of all the types of batting out there today. You can find blends of all the most popular batting fibers: cotton mixed with bamboo, for instance, or bamboo mixed with wool, or cotton mixed with polyester. There is even fusible batting which is coated with glue so you can iron the three layers of the quilt together before you stitch them.

Before you choose batting for a particular project, think about the climate where it will be used. In cool climates, use polyester or wool. For hotter climates, cotton or bamboo may be more comfortable and more resistant to bugs.

Also consider how much sentimental value this quilt will have. The more important a quilt is to you or the recipient, the more it makes sense to get a higher-end batting. But don't use silk batting for a preschooler's nap time quilt.

Ultimately, your choice is a matter of taste, use, and price. I urge you to try out different kinds of batting. Different fibers and even different brands make for a very different quilting experience.

Batting Sizes

Batting comes in the standard bed sizes: crib, twin, double, full, queen, and king. See the quilt size chart in Chapter 15 for more on choosing quilt and batting sizes for your quilt.

If the batting you have isn't just the right size, you can adjust. It's easy to cut down a large piece of batting to fit your quilt. You can also sew together smaller batting scraps to make a bigger piece of batting. To join two pieces of batting, butt the edges against each other and sew them together with a wide zigzag stitch. You can also iron a strip of lightweight fusible interfacing along the join to hold the two pieces together. Once the pieced-together batting is buried between the quilt top and backing, no one will ever know.

Quilting Tools

When it comes to making quilts, there are only a few tools you really NEED. There are lots of other tools you may want, but you can make a perfectly fine quilt without all the extra bells and whistles. As you gain experience, you will probably decide to add some other tools and supplies that make quilting easier and faster. This section covers the essentials and leaves the extras for later.

At the risk of sounding like a broken record, I want to say again that it's worth paying a bit extra to get high-quality tools. They can save you many hours of frustration and help you produce a quilt you can take pride in. Good tools will last for many years.

Chances are that you already have some of the items you need for quilt-making around your home, so it is worth taking stock of what you have before you rush out and spend your hard earned money.

Basic Tools

Sewing machine. You don't need a fancy machine, but your machine does need to be in good working order. It should be able to make a good straight stitch and hold proper thread

tension. Satin or zigzag stitches are useful if you are doing machine applique. A quarter-inch sewing machine foot designed especially for piecing is very helpful, if you have one. For free-motion machine quilting, you will want to be able to drop the feed dogs. Those are the little gears that pull the fabric under the needle while you sew. New machines have a button to do this. If you have an old machine, you may need to cover the feed dogs with a piece of cardboard for free-motion quilting.

If you've been making do with your grandmother's sewing machine, it's really worth checking out new sewing machines. They have all kinds of decorative stitches and labor-saving features Grandmother never even dreamed of, and the prices have never been lower. Like computers, sewing machines are one of those strange items that keep adding fantastic new features, while their price drops to almost nothing. There are many quilters who swear by their vintage machines and wouldn't trade them for anything. If you love all things vintage, an old machine may be for you. As for me, I'll take the modern conveniences.

Sewing machines need regular cleaning. Some need regular oiling too. Check your machine's user guide to see if yours needs to be oiled.

Whenever you change your needle (which you should do after every project, or after you use up two bobbins' worth of thread), remove the bobbin and clean the lint from the bobbin and needle areas. If your machine requires oiling, now is the time to do it.

It's also a good idea to take your machine in regularly for service. The more you sew, the more often you should have your machine serviced. Sewing makes dust build up in parts of the machine you can't reach. The more sewing you do, the more wear and tear and dust buildup you cause. A good sewing machine mechanic will clean everything up, correct the thread tension, and replace any parts that are getting worn. With proper care, your sewing machine should last for many years.

Sewing machine needles. Needles come in many shapes and sizes. You can get packets of

needles that are all one size, or packets with several different sizes of needles in them. There are a number of good brands and many specialized types of needles for different types of sewing.

I could write a whole dissertation on needles and how to match them to the different weights of thread for different kinds of sewing, but you don't need to know all that to make your first quilts. As a new quilter, you will only need two types of needles for two basic sewing operations:

- **Piecing.** To sew together the pieces of your quilt top, use a #80/12 topstitch or universal sewing machine needle. You will see the needle size and type on the front of the needle package. A topstitch needle has a larger eye than a universal needle, which makes threading the needle a bit easier. Either type will do the job, though.

- **Quilting and finishing the layers.** To machine quilt the quilt sandwich and sew on the binding, I recommend a #90/14 topstitch needle. A #90/14 needle is larger and stiffer than an

#80/12 needle. Using a larger needle helps you sew through all those layers without breaking your thread or skipping stitches. If you can't find a topstitch needle, a denim or quilting needle will also work.

Quilting tip: Don't try to see how long you can use a single needle – put in a new and unused one before you start each quilt. Worn needles get rough spots that can cause thread breakage and poke holes in your fabric.

Straight pins. You will use straight pins to hold layers of fabric together while you sew them. Pins designed especially for quilting are longer and thinner than all-purpose glass-head pins. I use the kind that has yellow balls

for heads. Some quilters prefer pins with flat heads that don't stick up above the sewing surface.

Iron. You will need an iron to press your fabric before you work with it. You will press the fabric again every time you sew a seam. Irons are the one exception to my rule that higher-quality tools are worth paying more for. I use a cheap iron I bought many years ago and have dropped on the sewing room floor a million times. It still works perfectly!

Do you need to use steam when you press your fabric? This is another one of those perennial quilting debates. Some quilters swear by steam, while others insist that steam distorts the shape of your quilt blocks and should never be used. Some quilters always starch their fabric before ironing. Some never do. Starch stiffens the fabric and makes it easier to cut and sew accurately. I use steam because it gets out more wrinkles than a dry iron, but usually don't use starch because I'm too lazy to take the extra step. Both ways are worth trying to see which one you like better.

Pressing board. You need a heat-proof surface to press your fabric. If you already have an ironing board, you can use that. I had my husband make me a pressing board out of a piece of plywood wrapped in a layer of cotton batting and a layer of cotton fabric. I put the board on my cutting table and press my fabric there. I like my homemade board because it is wider than a standard ironing board and feels more stable while I press.

Blue painter's tape. This tape is very useful for marking a ¼" inch stitching guide on your sewing machine bed, even if you have a ¼" quilting foot. If you don't have a quilting foot, blue painter's tape is really essential for sewing that perfect ¼" quilter's seam! One thing I like about blue tape is that when you're finished with  it, you just pull it off and it comes away without leaving a mark or any residue. You can find it at any hardware store.

Seam ripper. Even the best quilters make mistakes and have to rip them out. A good seam ripper only costs a couple of dollars U.S. It comes in handy when you discover you sewed something the wrong way.

Marking tools. If you need to mark your fabric, be sure to use a tool whose marks can be washed or brushed away. I recommend a silver Verithin™ pencil or a white marking pencil designed especially for sewing.

Cutting Tools

Scissors. A pair of good, all-purpose sewing scissors will come in handy for snipping threads and cutting off extra fabric tips. Make sure that the scissors are comfortable for you to hold and that your thumbs and fingers fit in the holes. I like the spring-loaded scissors by Fiskars, which do some of the work of cutting for you and fit hands of any size, large or small.

Rotary cutter. One of the great time-savers ever invented for quilters, a rotary cutter is the tool you will use to cut your fabric into the sizes and shapes you want to sew together.

Rotary cutters are measured by the diameter of the blade. Any quilt store or craft store will have cutters ranging from 18 mm to 60 mm. Large blades make it easier to cut large pieces and multiple layers of fabric. Smaller blades are useful for cutting curves or teeny little appliqué pieces. For general cutting, a 45 mm or 60 mm cutter works well. I usually use a 45 mm cutter.

The handles of rotary cutters are where the manufacturers get creative. You can get straight handled cutters, or handles that are ergonomically shaped to fit into the palm of your hand. If you do a lot of quilting, it's worth investing in an ergonomically designed cutter. That will help you avoid developing nerve and muscle problems in your hands.

Warning: the blade on a rotary cutter is essentially a razor blade, and it is SHARP. I highly recommend choosing a cutter that has a built-in safety feature that retracts or covers the blade automatically when you finish making a cut. If you have to remember to cover the blade yourself every time, you may forget one day and cut yourself. (Don't ask me how I know this.) Remember to always cut away from your body with a rotary cutter. Never cut toward yourself.

Cutting mat. You use a rotary cutter on a special plastic mat designed for cutting. These mats have a self-healing surface that allows you to cut again and again without gouging ridges in the cutting mat.

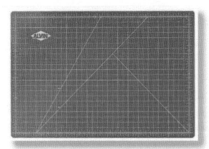

Cutting mats come in many different sizes, from little ones designed to sit next to your sewing machine, to big ones that take up a whole table top. I prefer a large mat that allows you to cut through a whole width of fabric at one time. Choose a size that fits on your work surface and into your storage areas. You can find cutting mats at craft and hobby shops or online.

Cutting mats for quilting come with pre-printed grids with every 1/8" and every inch marked. I find the marked lines very helpful for cutting, although the lines aren't always accurate. Use your ruler to make sure your measurements are accurate.

Never cut on a wooden or plastic surface because the cutter blade will score and damage the surface. Never iron on your cutting mat or leave it in direct sunlight, as that will make it warp.

Ruler. You are going to do a lot of measuring when you make a quilt, so a plastic see-through cutting ruler is an essential. If you only buy one ruler, I recommend the 6" x 24" size, which is long enough to cut a whole width of folded quilt fabric. Get a no-slip ruler—that will help you cut more accurately.

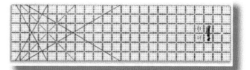

Basting Tools

Basting means holding the three layers of a quilt together temporarily so they don't shift or get wrinkled while you sew them together permanently. Basting is removed after you put in the permanent quilting stitches.

There are several ways to baste a quilt. This guide focuses on two methods: spray basting (the fastest and easiest) and pin basting (longer lasting, and better for those who don't like being exposed to chemicals.)

If you decide to spray baste your quilt, you will need a temporary spray adhesive that washes out after you finish the quilt. I use 505 spray adhesive from 3M, which is available at office supply stores and hardware stores. There are also a number of sprays made especially for quilt basting. You can find those at the quilting store.

If you want to pin baste your quilt, you will need safety pins. A lot of safety pins. The bigger the quilt, the more pins you will need. Regular safety pins aren't nearly as good for this job as the special large, bent pins made for quilt basting. Look for the stainless steel pins that won't rust. You can find them at chain fabric and crafts stores or at specialty quilting stores.

Tools for Machine Quilting

Most quilters these days opt to sew their quilt layers together by machine. If that's what you choose to do (it's my preferred method), you will want to have a few machine-quilting tools.

Quilting gloves. These are special gloves that cling to the surface of the quilt and make it easier for you to handle the quilt sandwich as you move it around under the sewing needle.

Walking foot. This is a special foot for your sewing machine that pulls all three quilt layers evenly under the needle. Without a walking foot, the top and bottom layers of the quilt tend to move under the needle at slightly different speeds, which can cause the layers to shift and get wrinkled. While a walking foot isn't strictly a necessity for your first quilt, it certainly makes machine quilting easier. Almost all modern machines will have a walking foot available. Older machines probably won't have one.

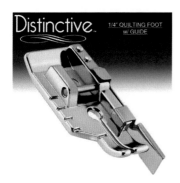

Tools for Hand Quilting

Most quilters today do all their piecing, appliqué, and quilting on a sewing machine. But a substantial number of quilters love the act of quilting by hand, just as their great-grandmothers did. Even some machine quilters use hand stitching to embellish their quilts or to sew the binding down as the last step in quilting. If you want to include hand work in your quilting repertoire, here are some tools you will need.

Thimble. Quilting by hand involves pushing the needle and thread through the fabric, over and over. That can be very hard on the part of your finger that pushes the needle. Thimbles protect that spot and keep you from developing blisters. There are all kinds of thimbles, from the old metal standby you may remember from Monopoly games, to leather thimbles with a  small metal piece at the spot where you push the needle, like the one shown here. Go to a fabric store and try on a few before you buy.

Hand needles. These come in various lengths and thicknesses, with eyes and points of different shapes to handle different stitching tasks. The needles called "Betweens" or "Sharps" are commonly used for hand quilting. Buy a pack of assorted needles and try the Size 9 needle to start. If that feels too large, you can move to smaller sizes. The higher the number on the needle, the smaller and finer the needle is.

Hand quilting thread. Look for a thread that is labeled "hand quilting thread." These threads are coated with a glaze that makes them easier to pull through the fabric by hand. Don't use them in your sewing machine! The glaze could gum up the works.

Quilting hoop. A hoop holds a section of the quilt taut to make it easier for you to stitch. Hoops come in many different styles and sizes, from small hand hoops for embroidery to large standing frames that take up a corner of your sewing room. To start out, try an inexpensive one from your local sewing store. I've had good luck finding hoops at the thrift store.

5/ Quilt Construction: Rotary Cutting

CAREFUL CUTTING MAKES your quilt pieces come out the right size. Properly cut pieces go together easily and lie flat when pressed.

Careless cutting produces crooked lines and makes your whole quilt come out crooked! This section covers squaring up your fabric, cutting strips, and cutting squares. These are the techniques you will use to make the quilts in later chapters.

If you're not naturally precise, learning to cut accurately takes practice. That's one reason why many quilters, me included, have welcomed the arrival of precut fabrics. Precuts are fabric pieces that have been machine cut by the manufacturer, so you don't have to square

up your fabric and cut it yourself. Precuts typically come as 2½" strips or 2½", 5" or 10" squares. New shapes and sizes are introduced all the time.

Each precut pack includes a set of several different, color-coordinated fabrics, usually all designed by the same designer. Use precuts, and you can make many quilts without doing any cutting at all!

Buying precuts is usually more expensive than buying fabric off the bolt and cutting it yourself. But many quilters think the extra expense is worth it.

Squaring up the Fabric Edges

If you are going to cut your fabric yourself, straightening the edge is a vital first step before you cut pieces to use in your quilt. Here's how to do it:

1. Start with fabric that has been washed and pressed to remove any folds and wrinkles.

2. Fold the fabric so the two selvages are together. If the fabric hangs perfectly flat

Fabric folded for squaring up, with selvages away from you

and you don't see a wave at the bottom near the fold, then fold the fabric again, lining up the first fold with the selvages. If you see a wave in the fabric, see the section below on Straightening Crooked Fabric before you cut.

3. Place the fabric on the cutting mat with the folded edge facing you. Line up the fold with one of the horizontal grid lines on the mat.

4. Put your cutting ruler so one edge of the ruler is about half an inch from the raw fabric edge. If you're right handed, put the ruler on the left edge. If you're left handed, put the ruler on the right edge. Align one of the inch marks on the ruler with the folded edge of the fabric. Make sure there is fabric under the ruler all the way from fold to edge.

5. Press down on the ruler with your free hand, as shown below. Keep your fingers open and arched so you are exerting firm, even pressure on the ruler.

6. Open the rotary cutter to expose the blade. Put the blade against the ruler, lightly touching the ruler's edge. Hold the cutter with your index finger extending down the handle toward the blade, as shown in the photo below. This gives

you better control over the cutter. With a long, smooth stroke and steady pressure, keeping the blade against the edge of the ruler, cut away from yourself.

7. When you have cut as far as the tips of the fingers holding down the ruler, stop cutting and walk your fingers away from you on the ruler. Press down with your fingertips again to stabilize the ruler.

8. Cut away from yourself again, keeping the rotary cutter blade against the edge of the ruler. Repeat as needed until you have cut all the way across the fabric.

9. Remove and throw away raw edge of the fabric. The newly cut edge should be at a perfect 90 degrees from the folded edge of the fabric.

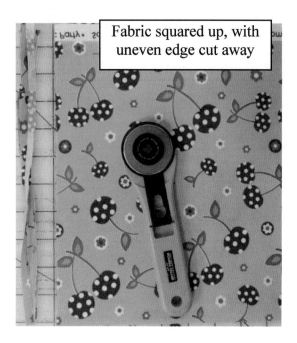

Fabric squared up, with uneven edge cut away

Straightening Crooked Fabric

If you see a wave or bulge in your fabric when you fold it, that means the fabric grain is crooked. You need to compensate for this before you cut, or you will end up with crooked strips. Here's what to do:

1. Fold the fabric in half so the two selvage edges are aligned with each other.

2. Hold the fabric by both selvages and lift it so the fold hangs down in midair.

3. Slide one selvage edge to the right, keeping the top edges of both selvages aligned with each other. Your goal is to make the wave in the fabric disappear. If sliding to the right doesn't make the bulge go away, or even makes it get larger, stop and slide the selvage the other way until the wave disappears.

4. When you have found a position that makes the fabric hang perfectly flat, with no waves or bulges, hold the selvages together without moving them and lay the fabric on your cutting table. The selvage edges on top should still be aligned with each other, but the side edges will be out of alignment. That's okay. Follow the instructions for squaring up the fabric edge, then you will be good to go.

Cutting Fabric Strips

1. First, square up the fabric as described above.

2. Put the ruler over the fabric so it covers the width called for in the project instructions. For instance, if the project calls for a 2½" strip, the 2½" mark on the ruler should be lined up with the cut edge of the fabric. Check the fabric fold to make sure the ruler is squared up with both the fold and the cut edge.

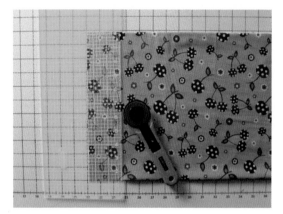

3. Cut the strip. If the cut is long, stop cutting in the middle, leaving the cutter against the ruler's edge. Then carefully walk your hand further away from you up the ruler. Press down on the ruler again and continue cutting.

4. Every few strips, recheck the edge and square up the fabric again if you need to.

Cutting Squares from Strips

5. Square up the fabric as described above. Cut a strip the same width as you want the square to be. For example, to make a 5" square, cut a 5" strip.

6. Lay the strip horizontally across the cutting mat. Align one edge with one of the horizontal lines on the mat. If the strip has a selvage edge, trim it away.

7. Line up the vertical mark on the ruler with the fabric edge so it covers a section the same width as the strip. The strip in the photo is 2½", so the ruler's 2½" mark is aligned with the edge of the strip.

8. Cut across the strip. The end result should look something like this:

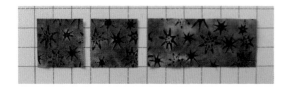

Troubleshooting Crooked Cuts

If your cuts don't come out straight, it's time to double check a few things.

- Have you sprayed the fabric with starch before ironing it? It is easier to make straight cuts in stiff, starched fabric.

- Are you using a no-slip ruler? They're much more stable when you're cutting than the other kind, which tends to slide around while you cut.

- Is the fabric edge really square? The fold and the vertical edge should be at a perfect 90-degree angle to each other.

- Is the ruler perfectly aligned with both the fabric fold and the cut edge?

- Are you pressing down firmly and steadily on the ruler with one hand while you cut with the other?

- Are you sliding the rotary cutter blade against the ruler as you cut? Are you pressing down on the cutter's handle with your forefinger?

- If you are cutting across seams, are you placing the units face down on the cutting mat for cutting? They will lie still and not slip under the ruler as you cut.

Remember, for most people it takes practice to become a perfect cutter. After many years of quilting, I still make lots of crooked cuts. That's why precut fabrics are such a boon for new quilters—experienced quilters too!

6/ Quilt Construction: Piecing

AFTER YOU CHOOSE your fabric and cut it into the proper sizes for the quilt you want to make, the next step is piecing the quilt, or sewing the fabric pieces together.

To become a good piecer, you only need to master one skill: sewing a scant ¼" seam. When you can do that, your quilt blocks will turn out the right size every time. Your rows will fit together perfectly when you assemble the blocks into a quilt. The tips of your stars and triangles will be sharp and pointy. Your quilt will lie flat when you press it. Everything will be great!

Getting Ready to Sew

Set the stitch length. Many modern sewing machines offer special stitches that have all the settings preset for piecing. If you are lucky enough to have a machine with one of these preset stitches, use the stitch recommended by your machine. If you need to set your machine's settings manually, I recommend setting the stitch length at 2.5, which gives you about 10-12 stitches per inch. Shorter stitches can be hard to remove if you make a mistake. Longer stitches may not hold your fabrics together firmly enough.

Preload a bobbin (or two.) There's nothing more annoying than running out of bobbin thread right in the middle of a seam. Before you start sewing, wind a bobbin with the same thread you will use in the top of the machine. Using the same thread helps you avoid thread problems. If you're making a large quilt, you might want to wind more than one bobbin.

Sewing a ¼" Seam Allowance

The seam allowance is the distance between your line of stitching and the raw right edge of the fabric you're sewing. One-quarter inch is the standard seam allowance used in almost every quilting pattern.

The seam allowance on a quilt block is hidden inside the quilt once you sew the block into a quilt. This means that the typical block is ½" smaller all around after the quilt is finished than it is before you sew it. Quilt patterns allow for this by telling you to cut the block ½" larger than its finished size.

The diagram below shows two pieces of fabric ready to be pieced, with right sides together and the seam allowance on the right.

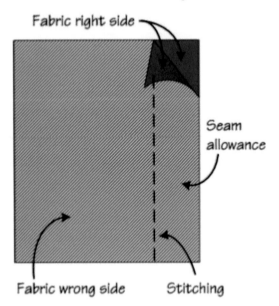

Quilters actually aim to sew a **scant** quarter-inch seam. This means aligning your stitching just a thread or two less than a quarter inch from the raw edge of the fabric. Why is this necessary? Because after each seam is stitched, the fabrics are pressed and folded off to the side. That fold uses up a couple of extra threads and shrinks your block just a little bit. You need to compensate by making your seam allowance a scant quarter inch. If you don't, your blocks will come out just a bit too

small. Multiply that by a quilt with many blocks, and the difference can really add up. Learn to sew that scant ¼" seam, and your blocks will turn out perfectly.

Here are a few tricks for achieving that perfect quilter's seam:

- **Use a ¼" quilting foot.** Most good sewing machines today offer a special foot that helps you sew an accurate quilter's seam.

- **Move the needle position to the right.** On many sewing machines, you can adjust the needle position to the right or left. I adjust my needle two clicks to the right of the quarter-inch seam setting. If you can do this, it is the easiest way to adjust your needle to the perfect distance for quilting.

- **Make a seam guide.** This is a line marked on your sewing machine bed that shows you exactly where to align the raw edge of your fabric. The ideal seam guide is thick enough to make an edge that guides your fabric along as you feed it under the needle. I use several layers of blue

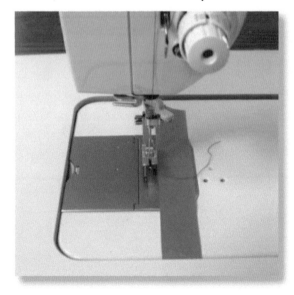

painter's tape. I do this even though I also have a ¼" quilting foot on my machine, because it helps me feed strips or longer pieces of fabric under the needle with just the right alignment.

How to Position a Seam Guide

1. Put your ruler under the sewing machine's presser foot.. Drop the needle until it touches a spot just a bit to the right of the quarter-inch mark, near the ruler's right edge.

2. Tape your seam guide to the sewing machine bed next to the edge of the ruler. Then you can run your fabric along the edge of the guide as you feed pieces under the sewing machine needle.

How to Test Quilt Seam Allowances for Accuracy

Here's how to check the accuracy of your seam allowances.

1. Cut three short, 1½"-wide strips of fabric.

2. Sew the three strips together, using a scant ¼" seam.

3. Press the seams to the sides, then measure the center strip. It should be exactly 1" wide. If it is too narrow or too wide, adjust your seam guide and check again.

Pressing After You Sew

Pressing is a vital part of sewing your quilt together. After stitching each seam, you will need to press the pieces you just sewed. I usually press the seam allowance to one side, so it is hidden under the darker fabric. This keeps the seam allowance from showing through the top of the quilt. There are some times when you may want to press the seam open instead of to the side. When a lot of seams met in one spot, pressing the seams open makes the junction less bulky for machine quilting later on. You won't need to worry about that for the quilts in this book, though.

When you press your work, always press the iron straight down and lift it up again to move to a new spot. Don't slide the iron sideways along the fabric, because that will pull your fabric out of shape.

Nesting Seams Together

Often you will find yourself sewing together two blocks or two rows where you are sewing over seams you previously pieced. In those cases, the goal is to match the seams so that when the quilt comes together, they look like perfect, uninterrupted lines. It really helps to press the seam allowances of the two blocks in opposite directions. This lets the two seams lock together in a way that looks perfect after you sew them. Quilters call these nested seams. They look like this from the side:

Pressing Alternate Rows to Opposite Sides

When you sew rows together, it helps to press all the seams in one row to the left, and the seams in the next row to the right. This makes it much easier to align seams perfectly. The seams in every other row of this quilt top (seen from the back) were pressed in opposite directions.

Time-Saving Techniques

You will get your quilt finished much faster if you do everything in batches. Cut a whole batch of the same strips at once. Sew a whole set of strips at once, then take the whole batch to your iron and press them all at the same time. Think of yourself as a home-based manufacturer, which is exactly what you are.

Chain Piecing

This is one of my favorite time-savers and thread-savers when I need to sew up a lot of similar pieces. Chain piecing is an assembly-line technique for batch-sewing a group of similar quilt pieces. It's very simple and easy to learn. Here's how to do it:

Sew from one block right onto the next

1. Start with a stack of quilt blocks or units you want to sew together.

2. Sew the first block. When you get to the end of the seam, feed the next block or unit under the presser foot so that it almost touches the first block. Sew directly from the first block onto the second one without cutting the threads or raising the presser foot (unless you need to adjust the position of the new block.) With practice, you will get very fast at this.

When you have sewed all the units, they will make a garland of quilt pieces, attached by a thin thread. Use your rotary cutter or scissors to carefully snip the threads between the pieces.

Squaring Up

As you cut your fabric and sew pieces together, tiny distortions inevitably creep into your work. This happens no matter how carefully you sew. Sometimes a block comes out slightly too small or too large. Sometimes the edges and corners get a bit crooked.

To make your quilt come out as perfectly as possible, you need to correct these little errors after each round of stitching. Quilters call this process "squaring up."

You will need your rotary cutter and a cutting ruler to square up your work. Here's what to do:

1. Carefully press the block or section you are working on. We'll call it a block for the sake of simplicity.

2. Lay the block your cutting table. Use your ruler to measure the block and check whether it is the size the pattern calls for, or larger or smaller than expected.

If the block is too small. A too-small block most likely means that your seam allowance was too wide. If this is the only block that is too small, the best thing is to pick out the seam with your seam ripper and sew it again with a smaller seam allowance.

If all your blocks come out too small, but about the same size, I would recommend deciding to love them at the size they are and sewing them together into a quilt. After that, you can work on achieving a more perfect seam allowance, as described in the beginning of this chapter.

If the block is too large. A block that is too big needs to be trimmed down to the correct size. Here's how to square up the block:

1. Place your ruler on the block, with one corner of the ruler at the corner of the block closest to you. If it's possible, align the ruler with seam lines inside the block so the outer edge of the ruler is located at the proper distance from the closest seams. In the photo below, I aligned the ruler to the two most recent seams.

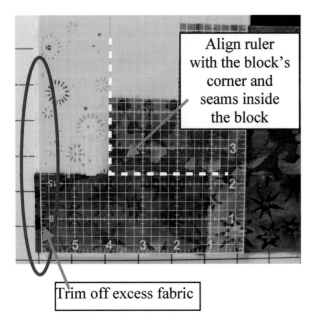

Align ruler with the block's corner and seams inside the block

Trim off excess fabric

2. Use your rotary cutter to trim away any extra bits of fabric that extend past the edge of the ruler.

3. Rotate the block to bring another corner close to you, then square up that corner. Do this until you have squared up all four corners.

Piecing Success Tips

Here is a grab bag of other tips to make piecing easier:

- Starch your fabric. Stiff, starched fabric makes cutting and sewing much easier. Use enough starch to make your fabric as stiff as a piece of paper.

- When you begin sewing a seam, start sewing on a small piece of scrap fabric (some people call this a "leader"), then chain stitch from the scrap onto your real quilt pieces. This helps avoid the ugly thread nests that can develop on the back of your fabric when you start sewing.

- Use a stiletto or a bamboo skewer to guide the fabric under the needle. This helps keep your seams nice and straight, especially as you get to the end of a seam.

- Keep your strips short. As fabric strips get longer, they are more likely to twist in one direction or another when you sew them.

- Reverse sewing directions as you add strips to a strip set. When you join two strips by sewing in one direction, sew in the other direction when you add the next strip. This helps keep your strip set from getting the bends as you add more strips.

7/ Quilt Construction: Backing and Basting the Quilt

A TYPICAL QUILT HAS three layers: The quilt top, which is the part you lavish the most time on; the batting, which is the middle insulating layer; and the backing fabric. This chapter covers how to put together the layers so you can sew them together permanently.

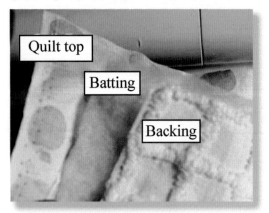

Piecing a Quilt Backing

The quilt patterns in this book are all small enough to be backed with one width of standard quilting fabric. You can skip this section until you decide to make a larger quilt.

When you do make a larger quilt that requires a bigger piece of backing fabric, here is a simple way to piece together a wider backing from two pieces of standard-width quilting fabric. This method works for quilts that are up to 80" wide.

1. Measure the length and width of the quilt top. Write down both measurements.

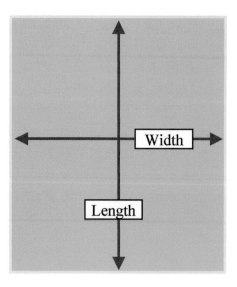

However big your quilt top is, your batting and backing layers should be a little bit bigger in both directions – a bit longer and a bit wider. The extra width gives you a margin of error that takes into account any unevenness in your piecing or shrinkage caused by machine quilting.

2. Cut two pieces of backing fabric. Each piece should be cut across the full width of the fabric (about 42") and 6" longer than the quilt's length. For example, if the quilt top is 50" long, cut two backing pieces that each measure 56" long by the width of the fabric.

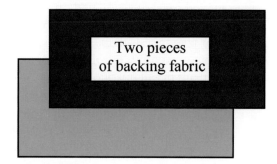

Two pieces of backing fabric

This gives you an extra 3" of backing at the top and bottom of the quilt.

The two pieces you cut can be from the same fabric or from two different fabrics. Mixing up the fabrics can be fun and also makes the quilt back look more interesting.

3. Cut one of the backing fabric pieces in half lengthwise, like this:

4. Sew the two cut pieces of backing fabric to the sides of the wider piece. Place right sides together when you sew the seams.

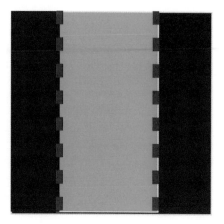

5. Center the quilt top and batting on the pieced backing fabric for quilting.

The pieced backing should be wide enough to accommodate a quilt top up to about 80" wide. You can make the overall backing narrower by by cutting down either the center backing piece or the side pieces.

Basting the Quilt

Basting is the process of temporarily fastening a quilt's three layers together until you can finish stitching them together permanently. You will remove the basting after the final quilting is in place.

While you can baste a quilt by hand with a needle and thread, the process is slow and laborious. I recommend two other methods:

- **Pin basting,** which involves pinning the layers together with large safety pins at intervals of a few inches all over the quilt top. This is the best method to use if you plan to spend months working on your quilt, or if you don't like to be exposed to chemicals. Spray basting is temporary and it definitely does put chemical fumes into the air of your sewing room.

- **Spray basting,** where you spray a temporary glue onto the layers to stick them together. After you finish quilting, you wash the quilt to remove the glue. This is my favorite method. It's the fastest and easiest way to baste. If you make a mistake, you can readjust the layers until they are perfect. One reason I prefer spray basting is that you don't have to handle safety pins. On a quilt of any size, pinning and unpinning can easily give you sore fingers.

Pin Basting

Here's how to pin baste your quilt:

1. Start by laying out the three layers to align them and make them as wrinkle free as you possibly can. Here's how to do this:

2. Cut the backing fabric so that it is at least 3" larger on all sides than the quilt top.

3. Lay the backing fabric, right side down, on the floor or on a large flat surface such as a cutting table or dining table. Smooth out any wrinkles. Stretch the fabric so it is slightly taut and smooth, but not drum tight. If you are basting on the floor, you can use blue painter's tape to tape down the backing at intervals around the outer edges. I usually baste on my cutting table and clip the fabric to the table with large paper binding clips.

4. Cut the batting about 1" smaller on each side than the backing fabric.

5. Put the batting on top of the backing fabric and unfold, smoothing out any wrinkles. Ideally, you should remove the batting from its package a day or two before this step to give it a chance to decompress. If the batting is very wrinkled, you may want to put it in a cool dryer for a few minutes. Once laid in place, you should see a rim of backing fabric all around the batting.

6. Lay the quilt top on top of the batting, right side up. Smooth it into place.

7. Using your basting safety pins, pin the three layers together at 3"-4" intervals all across the quilt top. Smooth as you go to keep wrinkles away. The basted quilt will look like this:

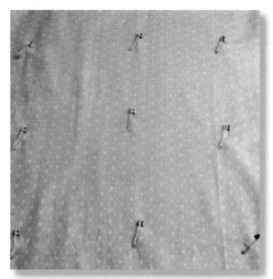

If you have a large number of pins to place, you may want to invest in a basting tool called a Kwik Klip that helps you place the pins without getting sore fingers.

Spray Basting

Caution: you should only use basting spray in a well-ventilated room. Here's what to do:

1. Cut the backing fabric so that it is at least 3" larger on all sides than the quilt top.

2. Lay the backing fabric, right side down, as described above in the section on pin basting. As with pin basting, you want the backing to be slightly taut and smooth, but not drum tight.

3. Cut the batting about 1" smaller on each side than the backing fabric.

4. Lay the batting on top of the backing fabric and trim to the size of the backing fabric. There should be a rim of backing fabric visible all around the batting.

5. Fold the batting in half so you can see half of the backing underneath.

6. If the quilt is small, lightly spray the whole exposed area of backing fabric with basting spray. If the quilt is large, spray a six-inch band of backing fabric just below the fold of the batting.

7. Carefully roll the batting down onto the sprayed area, smoothing any wrinkles from the center out toward the edges as you go. If you find any wrinkles you can't smooth away, pull the batting away from the backing and reposition.

8. For large quilts, keep spraying sections of backing fabric, rolling the batting into place, and smoothing, until you have basted half of the quilt. Then fold the unsprayed half of the batting back over the basted part and repeat the process on the second half of the quilt.

9. The next step is the quilt top. Lay the top on the batting the same way you laid the batting on top of the backing fabric. Fold the top in half so you can see the batting layer underneath. If the quilt is small, spray the whole exposed part of the batting. If the quilt is large, spray the batting in sections and roll the quilt top down over the sprayed area, smoothing as you go.

Once the layers are adhered together, they should stay that way for at least a month.

If you spray baste your quilt, make sure you wash it right after the quilt is finished. Washing removes the spray residue and eliminates the possibility that the spray might stain the quilt.

8/ Quilt Construction: Quilting the Layers

STITCHING THE QUILT'S layers together is a favorite step for many quilters. When you get this far, your quilt has started to look and feel like a real quilt. You can easily imagine what it will be like when it is finished.

Quilting the layers also offers tremendous scope for your creativity. For centuries, quilters have stitched spectacular feathers, flowers, and other fanciful designs into their quilts. The design in the quilt below, stitched by Olga Kuba, was created entirely with stitching!

For your first few quilts, I recommend something a bit simpler: stitching along the seam lines in your pieced quilt, and/or stitching all over the quilt in a regular grid pattern.

Check Your Batting

The type of batting you use determines how much stitching you need to do to anchor your quilt's layers together. Check the batting manufacturer's instructions to see how far apart they say your stitching should be. If you don't put your stitches as close together as the manufacturer recommends, the batting could shift and get lumpy when the quilt is used.

Old-time quilts had to be very closely quilted to keep the batting together. With today's modern batting, you can space your stitching much further apart.

Choosing Machine-Quilting Thread

A 40-weight quilting thread such as Aurifil or YLI is good for machine quilting. You can use the same thread in both the top thread and the bobbin. I use polyester thread because it doesn't shrink when washed and dried, but many quilters prefer cotton.

You can quilt with a thread color that blends in with your fabric and makes the quilting stitches less obtrusive, or you can choose a contrasting color thread that really makes the stitching stand out. The choice is a matter of taste.

On the first few quilts you make, your stitches may not be perfect enough to show off in neon colors. I recommend using a thread color that blends in with your fabric colors until you know your stitching is good enough to highlight. A thread slightly darker than your fabric will blend in to the background of the quilt. For the bobbin thread, use a thread that matches the color of the backing fabric.

Stitching in the Ditch

There's no better way to learn how to quilt than to stitch in the ditch. Stitching in the ditch means placing your stitches right next to an existing seam line in the quilt top. When you quilt this way, the goal is to hide your stitches in the little folds of fabric that run along the seams. Quilting in the ditch is a good way to practice making good stitches (if you quilt by hand) or sewing accurate lines (if you quilt by machine.)

I almost always start quilting the layers by stitching all of the quilt's major seams in the ditch, even if I plan to do other fancier stitching afterwards. Sewing along the seam lines anchors the quilt's layers so I can add more quilting without worrying about sewing wrinkles into the backing layer later on.

Stitching in the ditch

Quilting in a Grid

Another simple quilting technique is to stitch your quilt in a grid pattern. Use your ruler and a wash-away pencil or another marking tool, such as a strip of the ever-useful blue painter's tape, to draw vertical and horizontal lines every few inches across the quilt, then stitch right along the lines to anchor the layers.

As you get confident with your stitching, you can branch out and try some of the many more decorative styles of quilting. For most quilters, achieving smooth and even quilting takes a lot of practice. That's why I recommend a simple approach for your first few quilts.

The Rail Fence quilt below was quilted in a diagonal grid that gives a nice contrast to the vertical and horizontal lines of the Rail Fence blocks.

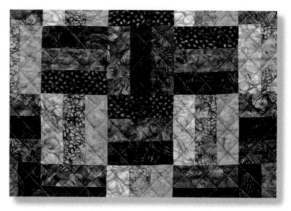

Machine Quilting

Here's the simplest way to machine quilt your layers together:

1. Wind a couple of bobbins with bobbin thread that goes with the backing of your quilt.

2. Put in a new 90/14 topstitch, denim, or quilting needle.

3. Set the stitch length on your machine to 2.5-3.0, or about 6-12 stitches per inch.

4. If you have a walking foot, use it now. Make sure to have the feed dogs engaged.

5. Put on your machine quilting gloves. I sometimes use just one glove.

6. Try a test seam on a quilt sandwich made from scrap fabric and batting. Check for loops of thread on the back of the test quilt. If you get thread loops, make sure that your needle is properly threaded and that the presser foot is all the way down before you start sewing.

7. Start stitching in the middle of the quilt, following the seam lines if you are stitching in the ditch, or following your marked lines if you're quilting in a grid. Work your way out from the center to the edges. This helps you smooth away any puckers that develop as you sew.

8. Anchor each new line of stitching by back-stitching two or three stitches at the beginning of the seam. Backstitch again at the end of the line. This will secure your quilting so it won't ravel with use.

Some quilters like to leave a long tail of thread at the end of each line of stitching, then go back later to thread the tails onto a hand needle and bury them inside the quilt layers. I prefer to do a good job with my back-stitching and trim the threads close to the quilt surface.

Hand Quilting

To quilt by hand, you only need one stitch: a simple running stitch. Here's what to do:

1. Hoop the section of your quilt where you will be stitching. Start stitching in the center and work your way to the outside. This helps you avoid wrinkles. Put the back of the hoop behind the quilt sandwich, then fit the front of the hoop over the front of the fabric. The layers should be smooth and fairly tight. After you have the hoop in place, push inside the hoop with your hand to create just a little give.

2. Make a small knot in the thread. Put the needle through the top and batting, but not into the backing, about an inch away from where you want to start quilting. Bring the point back up at the spot where you want to start. Pull gently on the thread and use your thumbnail to "bury" the knot, or help the knot pop in between the layers.

3. Stitch along the seam lines or the lines you've marked on the quilt top. Try to load several stitches at a time onto the needle. Quilting will

go faster that way. You will quickly see why you need a thimble!

4. When you get to the end of your thread, tie another small knot and bury it inside the quilt layers.

5. Pull the tail of the thread up firmly and snip it off, taking care not to cut the quilt top. The tail end will be hidden between the layers.

9/ Quilt Construction: Binding the Quilt

BINDING IS A double-folded strip of fabric that is sewed to the outer edge of the quilt to protect it from wear. An interesting or contrasting binding fabric also serves as a decorative element in your quilt.

You can buy premade quilt binding at a fabric store, but the colors and patterns available are very limited. Most quilters make their own binding from fabric strips.

Making Quilt Binding

To make your own binding, start with 2½" fabric strips. You can cut the strips yourself or buy them in strip packs at the quilt store. See the section on cutting strips above if you need help with cutting.

How Much Binding Do You Need?

Before you start cutting, you will need to figure out how much binding to make. To do this, measure the quilt across its width and length. Write down both numbers.

If you have a smart phone or tablet, Robert Kaufman Fabrics offers a free quilting calculator app called *The Quilter's Little Helper* that will calculate how much binding you need. The same app will also calculate how much fabric you need for borders and backings and do other useful quilter's math. There are other quilting calculators online, but I like this one because it is free and so easy to use. Using a special-purpose calculator is the easiest way to figure out how much binding you need.

If you want to do the math yourself, here's how:

1. Write down the quilt's length and width. Add 6" for trimming.

2. If the length and width are both less than 42" (which is the width of quilt fabric off the bolt), cut four 2½" strips across the full width of the binding fabric.

3. If any of the quilt dimensions is longer than 42", add the two numbers you wrote down, then multiply by two. For example: If your quilt is 50" x 60", you will need 220" inches of binding:

$$50 + 60 = 110$$

$$110 \text{ x } 2 = 220$$

Each binding strip is 42" long, so you will need to cut six strips of binding fabric:

220/42 = 5.238. Round up to get six strips.

Sewing the Binding Strips

Once you've cut your strips, you need to sew them together into one long strip.

1. Put two strips at right angles to each other, with right sides together, as shown below.

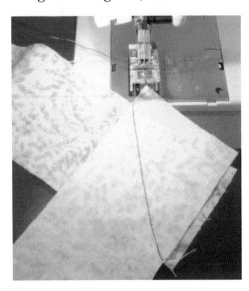

2. Pin the strips together (optional) and sew diagonally across the little box where the two strips are joined. You can see that my seam wasn't terribly straight, but the seam won't be visible once you finish the binding, so don't worry if yours isn't either.

3. Keep sewing strips together until you have joined all the binding strips into one long strip.

4. Use scissors to trim the seam allowance to 1/2". I usually throw away the little triangular scraps, but maybe you will think of something clever to do with yours.

5. Press the seams open. This minimizes the bulk of the seams. You will be glad of this when you sew the binding onto the main part of the quilt.

Binding strip seams pressed open

6. Fold the binding in half lengthwise and press it, taking care that the raw edges are perfectly aligned with each other.

Fold binding strip in half, press

Attaching the Binding to the Quilt

I've tried just about every method of sewing the binding to the quilt. Here's the one that I think is easiest.

1. Trim the quilted layers so the quilt is square and any extra batting and backing fabric are trimmed away. Put your ruler over each corner in turn to make sure they are all square.

2. Lay the quilt face down on your work table and put the binding strip on the outside edge, with the raw edge of the binding aligned with the outside edge of the quilt. Start with the end of the strip halfway down one side of the quilt where it won't be too conspicuous. Pin every few inches.

3. Sew the binding strip to the back of the quilt. Leave a tail of about six inches of binding

Sew binding to back side of quilt

unsewn before you start stitching. You will use that later to join the binding ends together. Use a ¼" seam allowance. Your quarter-inch quilting foot or painter's-tape seam guide will come in handy here.

4. When you get to a corner, stop sewing 1/4" from the corner. With the needle down, turn the quilt 90 degrees and back stitch off the quilt's edge.

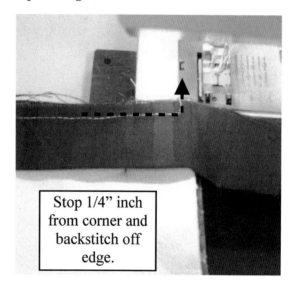

Stop 1/4" inch from corner and backstitch off edge.

5. Fold the binding up, then fold down again so it looks like the photo below, with a fold aligned with the top edge of the quilt and the binding strip aligned with the quilt's right edge. When you fold the binding to the front of the quilt,

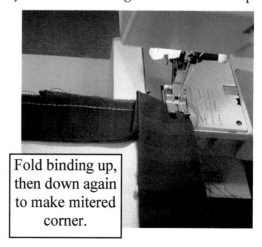

Fold binding up, then down again to make mitered corner.

this strange-looking arrangement will make a neat mitered corner on the front.

6. Keep sewing around the quilt, following the steps above at each corner. When you get back to where you started, trim the tails of the binding with scissors so the tail overlaps the beginning of the binding by about an inch.

7. Fold the tail end of the binding over about ½", so the raw edge is hidden inside the binding. Press the folded end.

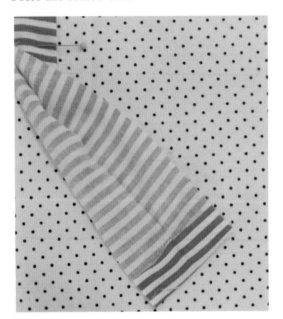

8. Insert the beginning end of the binding inside the tail, as shown in the photo below. Stitch the folded end down. (Note that this is a simplified method for you to use when you're just starting out. As you gain experience, you will probably

want to switch to one of the more elegant and more complicated ways to finish off the tail of your binding.)

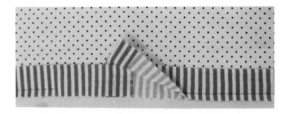

9. Next, you'll fold the binding to the front of the quilt. Put the quilt on your ironing board, back side up. Press the binding away from the quilt. This makes it easier to fold the binding to the front of the quilt.

10. Lay the quilt on your work table with the quilt top facing up. Pick one corner of the quilt and fold the binding into a mitered corner. The fold in the binding should run into the corner at a 45-degree angle. Pin the miter in place. Make sure the top fold points in the same direction as your sewing direction.

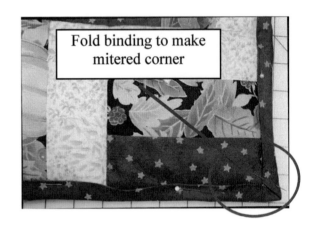

Fold binding to make mitered corner

11. Pin the binding to the front of the quilt along one side, making sure to maintain a consistent binding width. You can pin all along the side or use just a few pins and move them as you sew.

12. Machine sew the edge of the binding to the front of the quilt. I like to use my machine's decorative stitches to do this. Here's an example from a Halloween quilt. The jagged stitching goes with the quilt's spooky ghost theme:

   If your machine has decorative stitches, it can be really fun to try them out and choose the ones that match the theme and colors of your quilt. The binding is also a fun way to try out bold colors and prints.

10/ Project #1: Quilt-as-you-go Table Runner (15" x 54")

FABRIC REQUIREMENTS

- ¼ yard each of three or more different fabrics in coordinating colors.

- Backing fabric: 1½ yard. Choose any color that coordinates with the fabrics on the quilt top.

- Batting: one piece, 15" x 54"

- Binding fabric: 3/8 yard

O F ALL THE clever techniques quilters have developed to make quilting fast and easy, quilt-as-you-go has to be my favorite. The quilt-as-you-go method shortens the time it takes to make a quilt by turning the customary order of assembling a quilt upside down.

Instead of piecing the quilt top first, then adding the backing and batting and quilting the layers, this quilt-as-you-go table runner starts with the backing and batting fabric. You layer them together, then sew the top directly onto them, piecing the top and quilting the layers in one easy step.

This table runner is fun and easy to make, and it looks great when you're finished. You can use the same techniques you'll learn doing this quilt to make placemats, baby quilts, and any other small quilted project.

The beauty of the design is that it's flexible enough to use whatever fabric strips you have on hand that look good together. I used a mixture of strip widths for this table runner that included some 1½" wide strips, some 2½" wide, and some 3½" wide. You could also use all precut jelly roll strips (2½" wide) and save yourself the work of cutting.

I think this quilt looks best if you only use one or two large-scale or bold prints. Complement the bold patterns with solids and small-scale prints. I made this table runner with a blue-green palette and some bright reds, pinks, and whites for contrast. You could choose any set of colors that appeal to you. This pattern also makes a great seasonal quilt. You can see a detail of a table runner I made for Halloween on page 44. Here's how it might look with Christmas fabrics:

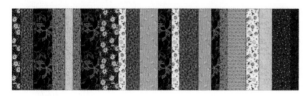

Batting for Table Runners

For table runners, place mats, coasters, or anything that needs to lie flat and possibly have hot dishes put on it, I recommend using a low-loft cotton, bamboo, or washable wool batting. Don't use polyester if you will be putting anything hot on the table runner. A too-hot dish might make the batting melt.

Cutting the Fabric

1. Cut the batting and the backing fabric to 15" x 54."

2. Cut the top fabrics into 1½", 2½", and 3½" strips. Here's how:

   - Fold the fabric with selvages together. Trim off the selvages.

   - Cut each strip across the whole width of the fabric, as described in the section on cutting above.

   - Cross-cut the strips into 15" sections.

3. Cut four 2½" strips of the binding fabric.

Sewing the Quilt

Make all seam allowances ¼". See the section on sewing above for more on seam allowances.

1. Lay the backing fabric right side down on your work table. Smooth the batting into place on top of the backing fabric. If you want to, you can use basting spray or temporary adhesive spray to adhere the batting to the backing. I find this isn't necessary for a small quilt like this.

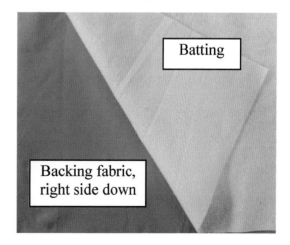

Batting

Backing fabric, right side down

2. Lay a strip of fabric on one end of the table runner, *right side up*.

First strip laid on backing, right side up

3. Lay the second strip on top of the first strip, *right side down*. Align the bottom edges together. Don't worry if a bit of fabric hangs over the edges of the batting and backing. You will trim them off later.

Second strip laid on first strip, right side down

4. Pin the strips a couple of times along the edge so they won't shift when you sew them.

5. Sew along the bottom edge of the strips, using a 1/4" seam.

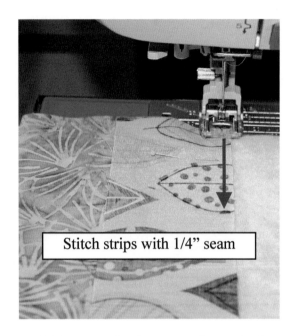

Stitch strips with 1/4" seam

6. Fold the second strip over and press it. You should now be able to see the right sides of both strips.

Press strips open after sewing

7. Keep adding strips in the same way until you reach the end of the table runner.

8. Use a ruler and rotary cutter to square up the corners of the runner and trim off the extra fabric.

9. Sew together and press the binding strips as described in the section on binding your quilt, above.

10. Sew the binding to the table runner as described above.

Now you're done! Put the quilt on the table and enjoy it.

11/ Project #2: Easy Rail Fence Quilt (36" x 48")

FABRIC REQUIREMENTS

- Light fabric: 5/8 yard

- Medium fabric: 5/8 yard

- Dark fabric: 1 yard. The extra 3/8 yard will be the binding fabric.

- Backing fabric: 1½ yard. Choose any color that coordinates with the fabrics on the quilt top.

- Batting: crib size piece or 40" x 51" piece of batting

THIS RAIL FENCE design is perfect for new quilters because it's easy to cut, easy to sew, and very forgiving of any mistakes you might make. Experienced quilters like it, too. I have made many Rail Fence quilts and never get tired of making them in new fabric combinations.

This quilt pattern calls for three fabrics: one light, one medium, and one dark. It's also a good idea to choose one small-size print, one medium-sized print, and one larger-scale print.

You can make this same Rail Fence quilt in many different colors. The quilt shown above has a cheery red, white, and pink palette, but you can make a completely different quilt by simply switching the fabric colors. Here's the same quilt in an autumn palette:

And here it is using blue, green, and yellow. See how different it looks if you choose two darker prints and one lighter one:

Cutting the Fabric

Cut the fabric into 2½" strips. Here's what to do:

1. Fold the fabric with selvages together, then trim off the selvages.

2. Cut each strip across the whole width of the fabric, as described in the section on cutting above. Here's what to cut:

*   8 strips of light fabric

*   8 strips of medium fabric

*   13 strips of dark fabric. The extra strips will be used to make the quilt binding.

Sewing the Quilt

Make all seam allowances ¼". See the section on piecing, above, for more on seam allowances.

1. Stack the strips into three piles, one pile per fabric. Arrange the piles as you want them to be in the finished blocks.

2. Sew the strips together into sets of three, adding one strip at a time. Each set will have one light strip, one medium strip, and one dark strip. Always sew with the fabrics' right sides together.

3. Press the seam allowances to one side after adding each strip.

4. When you are done sewing, you will have 8 strip sets. The completed strip sets should be 6½" wide. If yours turn out wider or narrower, write down the actual width. You will use that dimension in the next step.

5. Using your rotary cutter and ruler, cross cut each set of strips into squares the same size as the strip width. If your strips were a perfect 6½" wide, cross-cut the strip sets every 6½". If the strips were only 6" wide, cut the strips every 6". You get the picture: you want to end up with perfect squares – or squares that are as perfect as possible. You will need 48 squares to make the quilt.

6. Arrange the squares into a zigzag pattern with eight rows of six blocks each—48 blocks in all. Use the photo of the finished quilt from the beginning of the chapter as a guide for laying out the blocks. I like to have my blocks all arranged as they will be in the quilt before I start to sew them together. That way I don't accidentally turn them the wrong way or get them out of order.

7. Sew the squares together, one horizontal row at a time. Use a ¼" seam.

8. Sew the rows together into a complete top, one row at a time. Work from top to bottom.

9. Layer the quilt sandwich, then baste, quilt and bind as described in the sections on quilt construction above.

12/ Project #3: Double Four-Patch Baby Quilt (36" x 46")

FABRIC REQUIREMENTS

- White solid or print: 1 yard
- Pink print 1: ½ yard
- Pink print 2: ¼ yard
- Orange/pink print: ¼ yard
- Coordinating binding fabric: 3/8 yard
- Batting: 1½ yard
- Backing fabric: 1½ yard

THIS DOUBLE FOUR-PATCH pattern is a bit more challenging than the previous two, but still easy enough to be a fun first quilt. This design is built from two different blocks. The first block is just a plain 5" fabric square, in two different colors:

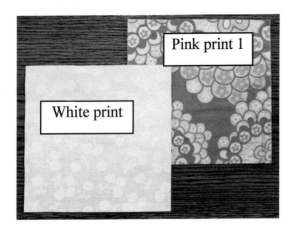

The second block is an old favorite called the four-patch block. The block has that name because it consists of four squares, or patches. This four-patch block uses three fabrics: Pink print 2, an orange/pink print, and the same white print you use for the larger squares.

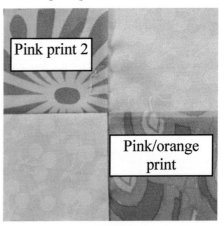

Combine two of the four-patch blocks with two plain fabric squares, and you have the double four-patch block, which looks like the photos below. This project includes two different double four-patch blocks, one white, and one pink. Here's the white one:

And here's the pink one:

For binding and backing fabrics, you can choose any fabric you like that coordinates with the colors on your quilt top. I like to bind my quilts with striped fabrics -- they help perk up any quilt.

For this quilt, since it is a baby quilt, you might want to use flannel for the backing fabric. If you do, minimize shrinkage by pre-washing the backing fabric at least once, and preferably twice.

Cutting the Fabric

To cut the squares for this pattern, you will start by cutting strips. Here's how to cut strips from your fabric:

1. Fold the fabric with selvages together, then trim off the selvages.

2. Cut each strip across the whole width of the fabric, as described in the section on cutting above. You will need to cut twenty 5" squares each from the white print and Pink print 1.

3. Cut three 5" strips of the white print and three 5" strips of Pink print 1.

4. Cross-cut all the strips into 5" squares.

5. Stack the squares in two piles: one white and one of Pink 1.

6. Cut the four-patch fabric into 2-3/4" strips. Here's what to cut:

- Six 2-3/4" strips of the white print

- Three 2-3/4" strips of Pink print 2

- Three 2-3/4" strips of the orange/pink print

7. Finally, cut five 2½" strips of the binding fabric.

Sewing the Quilt

Make all seam allowances ¼". See the section on sewing above for more on seam allowances.

1. Stack the 2-3/4" strips into three piles: one white, one pink, and one pink/orange.

2. Sew the strips together into sets of two. Pair one white strip with one pink or pink/orange strip with right sides together and sew along one long side of the strips:

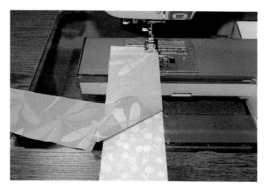

3. When you are done sewing, press the strips open.

1. Lay one white/pink strip set and one white/orange strip set together, with the colored strips on opposite sides. Try to rest the center seams against each other so they lock together.

Lay strip sets together like this

2. With the two strip sets together, use your rotary cutter and ruler to cross-cut each pair of strip sets into units that are 2-3/4" wide. Keep the pairs of strip units together after you cut them.

Cross-cut strip sets into 2-3/4" units

3. Sew along the long side of each pair of units.

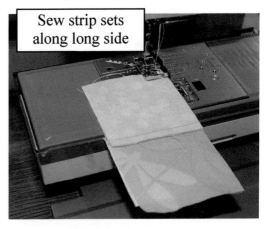

Sew strip sets along long side

4. Press the units open. You should end up with a four-patch block that looks like this:

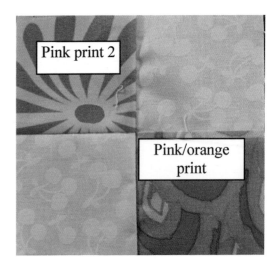

Pink print 2

Pink/orange print

5. Next, you will sew your squares and four-patches together into double four-patch blocks. Start by laying out the squares and smaller four-patches as they will be when the block is finished. For the pink double-four-patch, lay out the blocks like this:

6. For the white double-four-patch, lay out the blocks like this:

7. To piece the blocks, first sew the top two squares together, then the bottom two squares. You will get two rows that look like this. (When you sew the pink block, the larger plain squares will be pink.)

8. Sew the top and bottom rows of the block together.

9. The next part is the trickiest. Lay out your blocks, following the diagram on the opposite page as a guideline. It's easy to get a block or two turned around, so double-check your layout before you start sewing.

10. Now it's time to assemble the quilt. Start with the top row. Sew the blocks together, working along one row at a time. When you have five complete rows, sew the rows together, working from the top of the quilt to the bottom. I always pin the blocks and rows together before sewing to get the seam lines to nest together as perfectly as possible.

11. Layer the quilt sandwich, then baste, quilt and bind as described in the sections on quilt construction above.

13/ Conclusion

I HOPE YOU ENJOYED making your first quilts! In fact, I hope you enjoyed it so much that you will go on to make many more quilts in the future. With that in mind, I've put several charts in the following pages that I hope will be helpful to you as you make quilts of different sizes.

- **Metric Conversion Charts.** I know that many of my readers live in countries that use the (much more sensible!) Metric system. The next section includes two charts for converting inches and yards to metric measurements.

- **Bed Quilt Size Charts.** If you do much quilting, sooner or later you will want to make a bed quilt. This chart tells you how big to make it, and covers other factors to think about before you decide what size to make your quilt.

- **Table Quilt Size Chart.** How big to make that table runner? This chart will help you decide.

Please Send Me Your Questions

If you have any questions after reading this book, or if there is any way I can help you enjoy quilting more, please do email me for more information. I love to hear from readers. You can reach me at info@QuiltersDiary.com.

And Please Leave a Review

If you find that this book has helped you, I ask you to please post a review for others so they can get started quilting too. To leave a review, just visit the Quilts for Beginners page on Amazon.com and scroll down until you reach the button that says "Write a customer review." Click on the button to add your review.

Thanks for reading, and happy quilting!

Felicity

14/ Metric Conversions for Quilters

Convert Inches To Millimeters And Centimeters		Convert Yards To Centimeters	
1/8"	3 mm	1/8 yard	11.4 cm
¼"	6 mm	¼ yard	22.9 cm
1/3"	8 mm	1/3 yard	30.5 cm
3/8"	10 mm	3/8 yard	34.3 cm
½"	12 mm	½ yard	45.7 cm
5/8"	16 mm	5/8 yard	57.2 cm
2/3"	17 mm	2/3 yard	61 cm
¾"	19 mm	¾ yard	68.6 cm
1"	2.5 cm	1 yard	91.4 cm
1¼"	3.2 cm	2 yards	182.9 cm
1½"	3.8 cm	3 yards	274.3 cm
1¾"	4.4 cm	4 yards	365.8 cm
2"	5.1 cm		
2¼"	5.7 cm		
2½"	6.4 cm		
2¾"	7.0 cm		
3"	7.6 cm		
4"	10.2 cm		
5"	12.7 cm		
6"	15.2 cm		
7"	17.8 cm		
8"	20.3 cm		
9"	22.9 cm		
10"	25.4 cm		
11"	28 cm		
12"	3.5 cm		

Source: Craftsy.com

15/ Quilt Size Guides

THE CHART BELOW gives American quilt and mattress dimensions for bed quilts of all sizes, from crib to California King.

Keep reading after the chart to see other factors you should also consider when you plan how big to make a bed quilt.

Bed Quilt Size Guide			
Bed Quilt Size	**U.S. Mattress Size**	**Commercial Comforter Size (minimal overhang)**	**Bedspread Size (longer overhang)**
Crib	28" x 52"	36" x 54" For a toddler bed, make quilt 45" x 60"	N/A
Cot	30" x 75"	N/A	N/A
Twin	39" x 75"	65" x 88"	81" x 107"
Long Twin	39" x 80"	65" x 93"	81" x 112"
Double	54" x 74.5"	80" x 88"	96" x 107"
Queen	60" x 80"	86" x 93"	102" x 112"
King	86" x 80"	104" x 93"	120" x 112"
California King	72" x 84"	104" x 97"	116" x 116"

Other Factors to Consider When Sizing Bed Quilts

There are a number of things you should think about to make sure a quilt will fit your bed properly:

Mattress size. If you can, measure the actual mattress the quilt will go on. If you can't do that, use the mattress size chart on the previous page to estimate the proper quilt size.

Mattress thickness. Will the quilt hang down over the edge of the mattress or lie entirely on the mattress top? If it hangs down over the edge, it's important to know how thick the mattress is. Use these dimensions to estimate the amount of overhang your quilt will need:

Mattress thickness	
Standard	7" - 9"
Deep	10" - 15"
Extra-deep	16" - 22"

Mattress pad thickness. Many beds these days are topped with foam pads to make them softer. If there's a pad on the bed you're making the quilt for, use these dimensions to estimate the added depth:

Mattress pad thickness	
Standard	7" - 14.5"
Deep	15" - 22"

Box spring. If the quilt also needs to cover a box spring, add extra inches for the added overhang.

Pillows. If you want the quilt to fold up over the bed pillows, you will need to add extra inches to the quilt's length. If you can, measure exactly how deep the pillows are.

The most accurate way to estimate how much extra length you need is to make up the bed with a bedspread covering the pillows, then use a tape measure to measure from the tuck where the bedspread is folded underneath the pillows, up and over to the back of the pillows. Add this measurement to the quilt's length. If you can't measure, add 18" to the length for pillow coverage.

Quilt design. If your quilt features a central medallion or a central pattern, you may need to adjust your measurements to keep the center pattern from hanging down over the edge of the bed or getting hidden by the pillows. Often you can solve this problem by adding borders around the central design.

Density of quilting. How heavily will you quilt this top? The tighter your quilting is, the more your stitches will shrink the quilt top. Allow up to 5% of extra room in both width and length for shrinkage. Making the outer borders slightly deeper is a great way to do this.

Table Topper and Table Runner Sizes

How big should you make a quilt that goes on top of a table? The chart below gives dimensions for quilts to top several different size tables. Table runner quilts are a great way to try out techniques you're not quite confident enough to use yet on a bed quilt.

Table Type	Table Size	Table Topper/ Table Runner Size
Card Table	36" x 36"	36" x 36" Turn the table topper on the diagonal to put it on the table.
Dining Table: Small Rectangular	42" x 54"	13"-15" x 48" Center the runner on the table top.
Dining Table: Large Rectangular	42" x 72"	13"-15" x 72" Center the runner on the table top.

16/ About Felicity Walker

I HAVE BEEN QUILTING for nearly 20 years and have made dozens of quilts, but I still remember just what it's like to be taking those first steps toward becoming a quilter. making your first quilts.

I probably won't ever enter a quilt in a national show or win prizes for my fancy stitchery, but I love fabric and enjoy making easy quilts for my friends and family. I am always looking for simpler and faster ways to quilt. I have written several best-selling books for quilt lovers.

Now that we've gotten to know each other a little, let's keep in touch.

- Sign up for my free newsletter at my blog, **QuiltersDiary.com.**

- Follow me on Pinterest at **Pinterest.com/FelicityWbooks.**

- Follow Quilts for Beginners on Facebook: Facebook.com/QuiltsforBeginners

- Follow Quilter's Diary on Twitter: twitter.com/QuiltersDiary

More Books for Quilters by Felicity Walker

Rag Quilting for Beginners. Book #2 in the Quilting for Beginners series, this book shows you how to make your first rag quilts. Easy enough for absolute beginners, the book includes a complete, step-by-step guide to the basics of rag quilting: choosing fabrics, cutting, sewing, quilting, and finishing a rag quilt, with lots of photos and helpful tips to make everything easy, plus 11 fun and easy rag quilting patterns for beginners, each one with complete photo instructions.

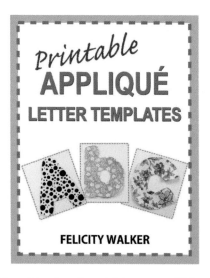

Printable Appliqué Letter and Number Templates. Sew raw-edged appliqué onto quilts, purses, pillows, shirts, dresses, hoodies… you name it! This little book of appliqué alphabet patterns makes it easy to personalize handmade fabric projects with names, words, or dates of special occasions like birthdays, wedding anniversaries, graduations. Includes a complete alphabet of uppercase and lowercase letters, numbers from 0 to 9, and a few commonly used symbols.

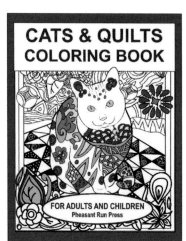

Cats and Quilts Coloring Book. 24 coloring pages featuring beautifully intricate drawings of cats and the quilts they love. Creative relaxation at its best for both adults and children. Perfect for markers, fine-point pens, coloring pencils, or crayons. Each coloring page is blank on the reverse side so colors won't bleed through.

Cats and Quilts 2016 Monthly Calendar.

We know who really rules the quilting room! 2016 monthly calendar features 12 cute, clever kitties snuggled up on quilts and in the sewing room. Includes U.S. National holidays. Slim 5½ " x 8½ " size is small enough to tuck into a purse or keep on your desk. January-December 2016.

17/ Photo Credits

The photos credited below were used with permission under a Creative Commons license:

Page Number	Photo Credit
6	Drunkard's Path quilt. Jennifer Worthen, Flickr.com
6	Appliqué flowers. A. Niza, Flickr.com
7	Baltimore Album quilt. gertvr, Flickr.com
8	A quilt for Katie. Essie, Flickr.com
9	Warm and cool fabric stacks. Gabrielle, Flickr.com
12	William Morris print fabric. Wikimedia Commons
13	Spools of thread. Gina pina, Flickr.com
12	Small rose print fabric. Tai O'Leary, Flickr.com
21	Cutting with a rotary cutter. Flickr.com
24	Girl at Sewing Machine, by Edward Hopper. Wikipedia.org
25	Fabric seam allowance. Wikimedia Commons
29	Quilt layers. ohsohappytogether, Flickr.com.
33	Quilted heart. Olga Kuba, Flickr.com
35	Hand quilting with thimble. Andrea_R, Flickr.com.
36	Quilt binding. Bjorn Hermans, Flickr.com.
40	Quilt binding. Dana, Flickr.com

23208506R00036

Printed in Great Britain
by Amazon